T0197487

it's Good To Be a Baby

Summer Rane

To order additional copies of this book, contact:
Xlibris
844-714-8691
www.Xlibris.com
Orders@Xlibris.com

ISBN: Softcover   978-1-6698-1446-7
        Hardcover   978-1-6698-1447-4
        EBook   978-1-6698-1445-0

Print information available on the last page

Rev. date: 03/03/2022

It's Good To Be A Baby

I see faces every day.

There is a Lady who loves to kiss babies.

There is a man who has trouble speaking. The only thing he can say is "Da Da."

There is a boy who is super cool. He gives me his toys to chew on. The Lady thinks this is not fun. "Look Out. Here she comes!"

There is a little girl with big curly brown
locks who is quite sure to be a doctor
one day. She loves undressing me.
Which causes the Lady to jump, scream, and
shout while wildly waving her arms about!

"WHO ARE THESE PEOPLE?"

I am four months old today and am happy
to say, I finally recognize the people
I see every day! They are my family!

It's good to be a baby. Months have come and gone. Today is my birthday! I am One!

"The next twelve months are sure to be FUN! As I learn to hop, skip, jump and run. Yes, I'm looking forward to being One."

The End

Printed in the United States
by Baker & Taylor Publisher Services